Tools for Problem Solving

Level E

STECK-VAUGHN
COMPANY

A Division of Harcourt Brace & Company

Acknowledgments

Executive Editor	Diane Sharpe
Senior Project Editor	Donna Rodgers
Editor	Allison Welch
Design Project Manager	Sheryl Cota
Cover Design	John Harrison
Electronic Production	PC&F, Inc.

Photography Cover: © Scott Melcer; p.6 Corel Photo Studios; p.9 © PhotoDisc; p.11 © Nancy Sheehan/PhotoEdit; p.12 Courtesy of the Library of Congress; p.14 ©Nancy Sheehan/PhotoEdit; p.20 © Superstock; p.24 (t) © Gabe Palmer/The Stock Market; p.24 (m) © PhotoDisc; p.24 (b) © Superstock; p.26 © PhotoDisc; p.32 © Photo Shot/ Bavaria/ Viesti Associates; p.33 © PhotoDisc; p.34 © Michael Newman/ PhotoEdit; p.35 © Superstock; p.36 (t) © M. Ferguson/PhotoEdit; p.36 (m) © Superstock; p.37 © Spencer Gran/PhotoEdit; p.40 (t) © Cathlyn Melloan/Tony Stone Images; p.40 (m) © The Stock Market; p.40 (b) ©PhotoDisc; p.42 © Michael Newman/PhotoEdit; p.43 © M. Ferguson/PhotoEdit; p.45 © Michael Newman/ PhotoEdit; p.48 © Kunio Owaki/The Stock Market; pp.49, 53 © PhotoDisc; p.55 Courtesy of Nancy's Notions, Ltd. (1-800-833-0690); p.61 © PhotoDisc; p.62 Park Street; p.63 © Jeff Greenburg/PhotoEdit; p.65 (t, bl) © PhotoDisc; p.66 (m) Quinn Stewart; pp.66 (b), 67, 69 (b), 70 ©PhotoDisc; p.71 © Martha Cooper/The Viesti Collection; p.74 © Tony Freeman/ PhotoEdit; p.75 © Lawrence Migdale/Tony Stone Images; p.76 (b) © PhotoDisc; p.77 (t) © Mark Gamba/The Stock Market; p.77 (b) © Robert Ginn/PhotoEdit; pp.84, 93 (b) ©PhotoDisc. Additional photography by Digital Studios.

Illustration pp. 4, 10, 13, 16, 18, 20, 21, 23, 25, 27, 28, 31, 43, 44, 47, 50, 51, 54, 63, 70, 73, 78, 80–84, 89–92 Dave Blanchette; pp. 22, 25, 29, 30, 38, 39, 41, 57, 73 Bill Ogden.

ISBN   0-8172-8129-0

4 5 6 7 8 9 10 PO 02

Contents

Magic Squares

Lesson 1   Write a Plan

This turtle has a square on its back. There is a pattern in the square. Any three numbers in a straight line have the same sum. Three numbers are missing from the square. What are the missing numbers?

Write a plan to solve the problem.

Step 1   Write in your own words what you need to find out.

_____

_____

Step 2   Write the facts that will be useful.

_____

_____

_____

Step 3   Explain or show how you will solve the problem.

_____

_____

_____

_____

_____

_____

Work Backward

Try working backward to solve the problem.

Each dot equals 1. Find the value of each design. Look for a row of three numbers. Find the magic sum. Then work backward from the sum. What are the missing numbers on the turtle's back?

1. Count the dots on each part of the turtle's back. Write the numbers in the grid.

2. Add the first row of numbers.

   _____ + _____ + _____ = _____

3. Add the middle column of numbers.

   _____ + _____ + _____ = _____

4. Add the diagonal from the top left corner to the bottom right corner.

   _____ + _____ + _____ = _____

5. What do you notice about these sums?

   _____

   _____

6. What are the missing numbers? How did you find them?

   _____

   _____

Practice

Here are three practice problems for you.

Quick-Solve 1

What numbers are missing in this magic square?

3		7
	4	0
1	6	5

Quick-Solve 2

What are the missing numbers in this magic square?

14	13	
19		11
12	17	16

Quick-Solve 3

How many dots should be in each blank square?

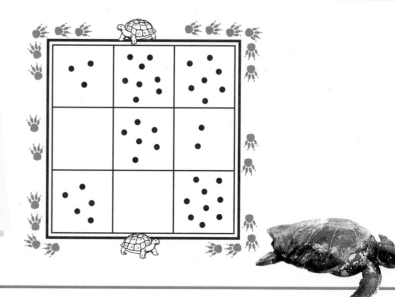

Use What You Know

Complete the magic square.
Four numbers are missing.
What are the missing numbers?

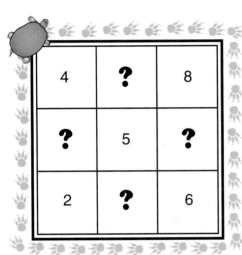

1. List the numbers from 1 to 9 that are not in the square.

   _____, _____, _____, _____

2. Use the missing numbers to complete the equations. Make 4 different equations.

   _____ + 5 + _____ = 15   _____ + 5 + _____ = 15

   _____ + 5 + _____ = 15   _____ + 5 + _____ = 15

3. Which equation above will work in the middle row?

   _____ + 5 + _____ = 15

4. Complete the magic square.

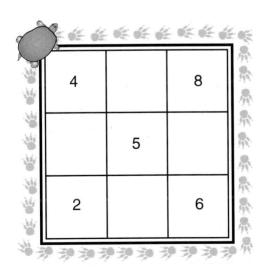

Lesson 2   Write a Plan

Another famous magic square has
4 numbers across and down.
Two numbers are missing.
What are the missing numbers?

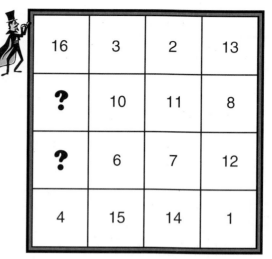

16	3	2	13
?	10	11	8
?	6	7	12
4	15	14	1

Write a plan to solve the problem.

Step 1

Write in your own words what you need to find out.

_____

_____

Step 2

Write the facts that will be useful.

_____

_____

_____

Step 3

Explain or show how you will solve the problem.

_____

_____

_____

_____

_____

Writing a Plan: Whole Number Operations

Work Backward

Try working backward to solve the problem.

> Look for a row of four numbers. Find the sum. Look for a column of four numbers. Find the sum. Find the sum of a diagonal of four numbers. Then work backward. What are the missing numbers in the square?

16	3	2	13
?	10	11	8
?	6	7	12
4	15	14	1

1. This square uses the numbers from 1 through 16. What numbers from 1 through 16 are

   not in the square? _____ , _____

2. Add the first row.

   _____ + _____ + _____ + _____ = _____

3. Add the fourth column.

   _____ + _____ + _____ + _____ = _____

4. Add the diagonals.

   _____ + _____ + _____ + _____ = _____

   _____ + _____ + _____ + _____ = _____

5. What is the sum of the numbers

   in each equation? _____

6. What are the missing numbers? _____ , _____
   Complete the magic square.

16	3	2	13
	10	11	8
	6	7	12
4	15	14	1

Practice

Here are three practice problems for you.

Quick-Solve 1

Add 3 to each number in the magic square. Write the sums in the blank square. Did you make a new magic square? How do you know?

1	14	15	4
12	7	6	9
8	11	10	5
13	2	3	16

Quick-Solve 2

What are the missing numbers in this square? How do you know?

	19	12
13		17
18	11	16

Quick-Solve 3

Subtract 9 from each number in this square. Write the differences in the blank square. Did you make a new magic square? How do you know?

17	12	13
10	14	18
15	16	11

Applying Strategies

Use What You Know

What are the missing numbers in the magic square?

1. Add the numbers in the first row.

_____ + _____ + _____ = _____

2. Add the numbers in the last row.

_____ + _____ + _____ = _____

3. What is the sum of the numbers in each equation? _____

4. Find the missing number in the first column.

20 + _____ + 10 = _____

5. What is the missing number in the middle of the square?

_____

6. How can you check that the middle number is correct?

_____

_____

Lesson 3   Use Logical Reasoning

You solved magic square problems by working backward.
Now try using logical reasoning to solve a problem.

Below are 3 magic squares that Ben Franklin and his
brother and sister might have made. Use the clues to
find the person who made each magic square.

When Ben Franklin was a boy, his
hobby was making magic squares.

Magic Square A

4	9	2
3	5	7
8	1	6

Magic Square B

8	1	7
3	5	6
4	9	2

Magic Square C

10	3	8
5	7	9
6	11	4

Clues:

- Ben's square had only even numbers in the corners.
- Ben's sister made a square with no numbers greater than 10.
- Ben's brother made a magic square that did not work.

1. Which squares have only even numbers in each corner?

   _____ and _____

2. Which squares have no numbers greater than 10?

   _____ and _____

3. Which square does not work? _____

4. Which square did each person make?

   Magic Square A _____   Magic Square B _____   Magic Square C _____

Using Logical Reasoning: Whole Number Operations

Practice

Here are three practice problems for you.

Quick-Solve 1

Is the missing number odd or even? How do you know?

5	10	3
4	6	8
	2	7

Quick-Solve 2

Is the missing number greater than 10 or less than 10? How do you know?

16	9	14
	13	15
12	17	10

Quick-Solve 3

Nick made a magic square. He said, "The sum of any line of numbers in my square is an even number." Which square is his?

Square A

6	11	4
5	7	9
10	3	8

Square B

7	8	3
2	6	10
9	4	5

Use What You Know

If you need help, look back to page 12.

Below are 3 magic squares made by Clint, Mike, and Karmen. Use the clues. Which square did each person make?

Magic Square A

21	16	23
22	20	18
17	24	19

Magic Square B

40	25	40
35	35	35
30	45	30

Magic Square C

55	41	57
49	51	53
45	61	47

Clues:

- Karmen's square has only odd numbers in the corners.
- Clint's magic square has numbers less than 50.
- Mike's square has only one number that is a multiple of 5.

1. Which squares have only odd numbers in each corner?

   _____ and _____

2. Which squares have numbers less than 50?

   _____ and _____

3. Which square has only one number that is a
   multiple of 5? _____

4. Which square did each person make?

   Magic Square A _____

   Magic Square B _____

   Magic Square C _____

Using Logical Reasoning: Whole Number Operations

Lesson 4 Solve It Your Way

Read each problem and decide how you will find the solution.

You may choose one of these strategies for each problem.

Work Backward
Use Logical Reasoning

1. Find the missing number.

10	17	12
15		11
14	9	16

2. Subtract 30 from each number in this magic square. Is the new square a magic square? How do you know?

38	45	40			
43	41	39			
42	37	44			

3. Jane used the numbers 25, 5, 20, and 10 in the first row of a magic square. The first and last squares are multiples of 10. The number in the third square is half the value of the first square. Twenty is not in the first square. In what order did she write the numbers?

4. Find the missing numbers in the magic square.

11	18		23
24		17	12
25	20	16	13
14		19	

Practice

Here are three practice problems for you.

Quick-Solve 1

Use the clues to make your own magic square. Then share it with a friend.
- The magic sum is 51.
- The middle number is 34 less than the magic sum.
- The corner numbers are even.
- The numbers range from 13 to 21.

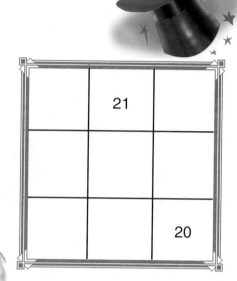

	21	
		20

Quick-Solve 2

Use the clues to make your own magic square. Then share it with a friend.
- The magic sum is 84.
- The middle number is $\frac{1}{3}$ of the magic sum.
- The numbers are all multiples of 2.
- The numbers 26 and 30 are each used twice.

		30
26		

Quick-Solve 3

Use the clues to make your own magic square. Then share it with a friend.
- The magic sum is 63.
- The numbers range from 17 to 25.
- The corner numbers are even.

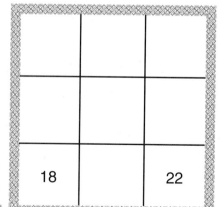

18		22

Applying Strategies

Review   Show What You Know

Work in a small group. Start with this magic square.
Change it 2 different ways.

7	0	5
2	4	6
3	8	1

1. Add 2 to each number in the square.
   Write your new square below.

   Is it a magic square?
   How do you know?

   _____

   _____

2. Multiply each number in the square above
   by 2. Write your new square below.

   Is it a magic square?
   How do you know?

   _____

   _____

3. Find the answers to the number clues
   to complete the magic square.

Clues	
10 − 5 − 1	10 + 5 − 1
10 − 5 + 1	10 + 5
10 − 5	10 + 5 + 1

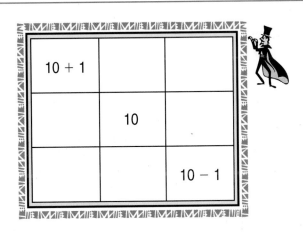

10 + 1		
	10	
		10 − 1

UNIT 2 Life on the Frontier

Lesson 1 Write a Plan

Suppose the year is 1788. Your family is floating down the Ohio River on a flatboat. You travel 30 miles each day. After 21 days, how many miles will you have traveled?

Write a plan to solve the problem.

Step 1   Write in your own words what you need to find out.

_____

_____

Step 2   Write the facts that will be useful.

_____

_____

Step 3   Explain or show how you will solve the problem.

_____

_____

_____

_____

_____

Writing a Plan: Multiplication and Division

Choose the Operation

Try choosing the operation to solve the problem.

> Multiply and divide the numbers in the problem. Look at both solutions. Read the problem again. Check which solution is reasonable. If you travel 30 miles each day, how many miles will you travel in 21 days?

Multiply to combine equal groups. Divide to separate equal groups.

1. If you multiply, what answer do you get?

$$\begin{array}{r} 30 \\ \times 21 \\ \hline \end{array}$$

2. If you divide, what answer do you get?

$$21\overline{)30}$$

3. Read the problem again. Does the answer make more sense when you multiply or when you divide? How do you know?

_____

_____

4. Can you solve the problem by adding? Explain how it might be done.

_____

_____

5. How many miles will the flatboat travel in 21 days? Is the solution found by multiplying or by dividing? Explain why.

_____

_____

Practice

Here are three practice problems for you.

Quick-Solve 1

Suppose your flatboat traveled 350 miles in 10 days. What was the average distance traveled each day?

Quick-Solve 2

A flatboat was narrow so that it could pass through narrow channels in the river. A typical flatboat was 50 feet long and only 15 feet wide. What was the area of a typical flatboat?
Hint: Area = length x width.

Quick-Solve 3

You are tired of riding on a flatboat with horses, pigs, and cows! Your father says that you will stop in 3 days when you reach Cincinnati. That is 72 miles away. About how many miles will you travel each day?

Use What You Know

When the wind is blowing with it, a flatboat
can travel up to 50 miles per day. What is the
farthest distance a flatboat can travel in 14 days?

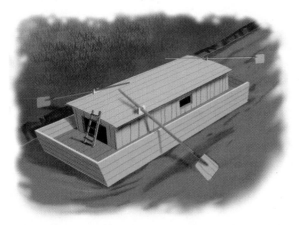

> Multiply and divide the numbers in the problem.
> Try to decide which solution is reasonable.

1. If you multiply, what answer do you get?

$$\begin{array}{r} 50 \\ \times 14 \\ \hline \end{array}$$

2. If you divide, what answer do you get?

$$14\overline{)50}$$

3. Read the problem again. Does the answer make more sense
when you multiply or when you divide? How do you know?

_____

_____

4. When the wind is blowing against it, a flatboat can travel only
30 miles per day at most. How far could a flatboat travel against
the wind in 14 days?

_____

5. Suppose the wind was with the flatboat for 3 days. Then it blew
against it for 2 days. About how many miles could it travel?

_____

Lesson 2   Write a Plan

In 1785, Congress sold land in the Northwest Territory for $640.00 per square mile. Suppose 4 families buy 1 square mile to share. If each pays the same amount, how much will each family pay?

Write a plan to solve the problem.

Step 1   Write in your own words what you need to find out.

_____

_____

Step 2   Write the facts that will be useful.

_____

_____

Step 3   Explain or show how you will solve the problem.

_____

_____

_____

_____

_____

Choose the Operation

Try choosing the operation to solve the problem.

> Multiply and divide. Check which solution is reasonable. How much will each family pay if they share the cost equally?

1. If you multiply, what answer do you get?

$$\begin{array}{r} \$640.00 \\ \times \quad 4 \\ \hline \end{array}$$

2. If you divide, what answer do you get?

$$4\overline{)\,\$640.00}$$

3. Read the problem again. Does the answer make more sense when you multiply or when you divide? How do you know?

_____

_____

4. Can you solve the problem by using a calculator? Explain the steps you would use.

_____

_____

5. Suppose 5 families want to share the cost of one square mile equally. A square mile costs $640.00.

How much would each family pay? _____

Practice

Here are three practice problems for you.

Quick-Solve 1

In 1785, land cost $640.00 for one square mile. How much land could you have purchased with $1,920.00?

Quick-Solve 2

Eight brothers want to share four square miles of land at $640.00 per square mile. How much will each brother pay if they share the cost equally?

Quick-Solve 3

Benjamin's grandfather was a gold miner. He gave Benjamin enough gold to buy 2 square miles of land. The land cost $640.00 per square mile. How much was the gold worth?

Applying Strategies

Use What You Know

One busy day the land office sold 9 square miles of land to 9 farmers. Each farmer paid $640.00. How much money did the land office collect?

> Multiply and divide the numbers in the problem. Try to decide which solution is reasonable.

1. If you multiply, what answer do you get?

$$\begin{array}{r} \$640.00 \\ \times \quad\quad 9 \\ \hline \end{array}$$

2. If you divide, what answer do you get?

$$9\overline{)\$640.00}$$

3. Read the problem again. Does the answer make more sense when you multiply or when you divide? How do you know?

_____

_____

4. Can you solve the problem by using a calculator? Explain the steps you would use.

_____

_____

5. One of the farmers plans to sell half of his square mile to his brother. If they share the cost of the square mile equally,

how much will the brother pay? _____

Lesson 3 Solve Multi-Step Problems

Now you will choose an operation for each step of the problem.

Ten farmers plan to buy 6 square miles of land to share equally. Each square mile costs $640.00. Don has 18 gold pieces that are worth $20.00 each. Does he have enough gold to pay for his share?

1. Find the total cost of all the land that the farmers will buy. Show your work.

   The total cost for 6 square miles is $————.

2. Find the amount that each farmer will pay. Show your work.

   Each farmer will pay $————.

3. Now calculate the value of Don's gold. Show your work.

   Don's 18 gold pieces are worth $————.

4. Review your answers. Does Don have enough gold to pay for his share? Explain how you know.

   _____

   _____

5. Don's sister gives him two more pieces of gold. Can Don pay his share of the land now? Explain.

   _____

   _____

Solving Multi-Step Problems: Multiplication and Division

Practice

Here are three practice problems for you.

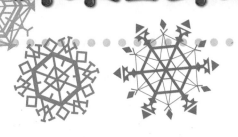

Quick-Solve 1

In 1785, Congress made laws to settle the Northwest Territory. Each town was made up of 6 sections. Each section was 640 acres. How much less than 4,000 acres was each town?

Quick-Solve 2

An old diary showed a record of 169 flatboats that passed down a river during two months in 1788. Each flatboat had 2 cows on it. The number of horses was 4 times the number of cows. How many cows in all were there? How many horses in all?

Quick-Solve 3

Another old diary showed a record of 1,608 horses that were moved on flatboats during certain months in 1788. There were half as many cows as horses. There were half as many flatboats as cows. How many flatboats were there? How many cows? What was the average number of horses on each of these flatboats?

Use What You Know

Now try solving another multi-step problem. Show your work.

Lewis and Clark took 68 days to reach the mouth of the Platte River. They rowed against the current and traveled only about 9 miles per day. On the return trip, they rowed with the current and went 70 to 80 miles per day. How many days shorter was their return trip?

1. How many miles did Lewis and Clark travel to reach the mouth of the Platte River?

2. If they traveled 80 miles each day, how long did the return trip take? Round up to the nearest whole number.

3. If they traveled 70 miles each day, how long did the return trip take? Round up to the nearest whole number.

4. About how many days shorter was the return trip than the trip against the current if they traveled 70 miles per day? 80 miles per day?

5. How can you estimate miles per hour on the return trip? Write a plan for finding out. Then write your estimate. Hint: You will have to estimate how many hours you think they traveled each day.

Solving Multi-Step Problems: Multiplication and Division

Lesson 4   Solve It Your Way

Read each problem and decide how you will find the solution.

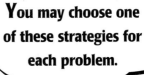

You may choose one of these strategies for each problem.

Choose the Operation
Solve Multi-Step Problems

1. Harry has 4 gold pieces. Each piece is worth $20.00. He also has $18.00 in coins. How much money does he have in gold and coins?

2. A farmer and his wife own 1,200 acres of land. They plan to divide their land equally among their 8 children. How many acres will each child receive?

3. The Erie Canal joined the West to New York Harbor. The men who built the canal earned $0.80 a day. If a man worked for 30 days, how much did he earn?

4. In the late 1700s, a family moving west would take cows with them to provide milk. If they got 21 quarts of milk each week, how many quarts of milk did they get each day?

5. Suppose that a family starts their flatboat journey on the morning of May 19. They travel 40 miles each day. How far will they travel by the morning of May 31?

6. If a family travels 184 miles in 6 days on a flatboat, what is the average number of miles they travel each day on the river? Round to the nearest whole number.

Practice

Now write your own problems.

Quick-Solve 1

The answer to a problem is "3 days." What might the question be? Write your own problem to share with a friend. If your friend does not get an answer of 3 days, discuss how you might change the problem or the solution to match.

Quick-Solve 2

The answer to a problem is "$320.00." What might the question be? Write your own problem to share with a friend. If your friend does not get an answer of $320.00, discuss how you might change the problem or the solution to match.

Quick-Solve 3

The answer to a problem is "200 miles." What might the question be? Write your own problem to share with a friend. If your friend does not get an answer of 200 miles, discuss how you might change the problem or the solution to match.

Applying Strategies

Review   Show What You Know

Work in a small group. Fill in the missing measurements in the chart below.

At the end of a trip, the flatboat was taken apart. Then the wood was used to build something else. Find the total number of square feet of wood on this flatboat.

Remember:
Area = length × width.

Wood from the Flatboat

Source	Length (feet)	Width or Height	Area
Base		15 feet	750 square feet
Front wall of cabin	10 feet	6 feet	
Back wall of cabin	10 feet	6 feet	
Left wall of cabin	30 feet	6 feet	
Right wall of cabin	30 feet		180 square feet
Roof of cabin		10 feet	300 square feet

1. What is the total area of the cabin wood? _____

2. What is the total area of all the flatboat wood? _____

3. Suppose a family sold the wood from this flatboat for $0.35 a square foot. How much money would they get? If they used half the wood and sold half, how much money would they get? Explain how you find the answer.

_____

_____

Review   Units 1–2

Read each problem and decide how you will find the solution.

Work Backward
Use Logical Reasoning
Choose the Operation
Solve Multi-Step Problems

Wow!
You can choose from all these strategies!

1. Sarah buys 4 square miles of land. Meg buys 3 square miles, and Ben buys 6 square miles of land. If the land costs $640.00 per square mile, how much did they spend together?

2. Nate got 3 more eggs than Ann. Ann got 4 fewer eggs than Tom. Tom got $\frac{1}{8}$ of the eggs. If the family's chickens laid 48 eggs, how many eggs did Nate have?

3. The sum in a 3 × 3 magic square is 180. One diagonal has the numbers 68 and 52 in the corners. Another diagonal has the numbers 53 and 67 in the corners. What is the number in the middle of the magic square?

4. A diagonal in a 3 × 3 magic square has numbers 15 and 25 in the corners. The center number is 20. One of the corner numbers in the other diagonal is 21. What are the other two numbers in this diagonal?

5. A family went downstream on a canal boat. They traveled for 5 days. They averaged 33 miles per day. How many miles did they travel?

6. One farmer gave each of his 5 children an equal share of his land. He started with 1,750 acres and kept 150 acres for himself. How much land did each child receive?

Cumulative Review: Applying Strategies

7. If land costs $640 per square mile, what would 6 square miles cost?

8. There are 640 acres in 1 square mile. How many acres are in a square plot of land that is 4 miles by 4 miles?

9. When the Erie Canal was finished in 1825, the first boat went from Buffalo to New York City in 6 days. The distance was 523 miles. What was the average distance traveled per day?

10. Joe Smith worked on the Erie Canal for $0.80 per day. He paid $0.25 per day for food and lodging. What did he earn in 45 days after expenses?

11. Some flatboats line up to pass through a narrow channel. The Trist's boat is between the Sand's and Adams's boats. The Kane's boat is first, just ahead of the Sand's boat. Whose boat is last to pass through the channel?

12. In 1791, Andrew Ellicott and Benjamin Banneker surveyed land for the new capital, Washington, D.C. The land was 10 miles wide and 10 miles long. How many square miles did they survey? Hint: Area = length $\times$ width.

13. Fill in the missing numbers in this magic square.

26	13		23
15		21	18
	16		22
14	25	24	11

14. Mark writes 22, 28, 48, and 50 in one row of a magic square. The corners contain a number with an 8. The third number is the sum of the first and second numbers. In what order does Mark write the numbers?

See How They Go!

Lesson 1 Write a Plan

A sports car can go 21 miles on one gallon of gasoline.
About how far can it go on 13 gallons of gasoline?

Write a plan to solve the problem.

Step 1 Write in your own words what you need to find out.

_____

_____

Step 2 Write the facts that will be useful.

_____

_____

_____

Step 3 Explain or show how you will solve the problem.

_____

_____

_____

_____

_____

Make an Estimate

Try making an estimate to solve the problem.

> The word *about* means an exact answer is not needed.

Estimate by rounding the number of miles and the number of gallons to the nearest 10. About how far can a sports car go on 13 gallons of gasoline?

1. Round each number to the nearest ten.

Actual	Estimated
21 miles per gallon	about _____ miles per gallon
13 gallons of gas	about _____ gallons of gas

2. Multiply the estimates. About how far can the sports car go on about 13 gallons of gasoline?

about _____ miles

3. Suppose the sports car could hold 21 gallons of gasoline. About how far could it go on one tank of gasoline?

$$21 \quad \times \quad 21 \quad =$$

about _____ × _____ = about _____ miles

4. Suppose you want to drive 500 miles in a car that gets about 18 miles to each gallon. About how many gallons of gas will you need? If your car has a 21-gallon gas tank, will you be able to make the whole trip without stopping for gasoline? How do you know?

_____

_____

Practice

Here are three practice problems for you.

Quick-Solve 1

A full-size truck can go 13 miles on one gallon of gas. About how many miles can it go on 12 gallons of gasoline?

Quick-Solve 2

Tamara's mom drives a mid-sized car. It gets 22 miles per gallon of gasoline. About how many miles can they drive on 11 gallons of gas?

Quick-Solve 3

A station wagon gets 19 miles per gallon in city traffic. It gets 28 miles per gallon in highway traffic. About how many more miles can you drive the station wagon on the highway than in the city if you have 9 gallons of gas?

Applying Strategies

Use What You Know

Brenna has a small car that has an 11-gallon gas tank. It gets 33 miles per gallon of gas. Riko has a sport utility vehicle in which the gas tank holds 23 gallons of gas. It can go only 13 miles on one gallon of gas. Which car can go farther on one tank of gas?

> Estimate by rounding the number of miles and the number of gallons to the nearest 10. Which can go farther?

1. What must you multiply to find how far each vehicle can travel on one tank of gasoline?

   _____

2. Estimate how far Brenna's car can go on one tank of gas.

   11 × 33 =
   ↓   ↓

   about _____ × _____ = about _____ miles

3. Estimate how far Riko's car can go on one tank of gas.

   23 × 13 =
   ↓   ↓

   about _____ × _____ = about _____ miles

4. Whose vehicle can travel farther on one tank of gas? _____

5. Are your estimates greater than or less than the exact number of miles each vehicle can travel? Explain.

   _____

   _____

Lesson 2   Write a Plan

Tom and his friends are going to a camp in the mountains. The camp is 237 miles away. His dad's sport utility vehicle gets 12 miles per gallon of gasoline. About how many gallons of gasoline will they need to drive to the camp?

Write a plan to solve the problem.

Step 1   Write in your own words what you need to find out.

_____

_____

Step 2   Write the facts that will be useful.

_____

_____

_____

Step 3   Explain or show how you will solve the problem.

_____

_____

_____

_____

_____

Writing a Plan: Multiplication and Division

Make an Estimate

Try making an estimate to solve the problem.

> **D**ivide to find the number of gallons of gasoline they will need.

Estimate by rounding the numbers so they are easier to divide. About how many gallons of gasoline will they need to drive to the camp?

1. Round each number to the nearest 10.

Actual	Estimated
237 miles to travel	about _____ miles to travel
12 miles per gallon	about _____ miles per gallon

2. Divide the estimates of total miles to travel by the miles per gallon. About how many gallons of gasoline will they use?

   about _____ gallons

3. What if you round 237 to the nearest hundred instead? What would the estimated gallons be then?

   237 ÷ 12 =

   about _____ ÷ _____ = about _____ gallons

4. Which estimate is more reliable, rounding to the nearest hundred or to the nearest ten? Explain why.

   _____

5. Tammy, a counselor, is also driving to the camp. Her car can go 26 miles on one gallon of gas. She will travel 296 miles to the camp. About how many gallons of gasoline will she need?

   296 ÷ 26 =

   about _____ ÷ _____ = about _____ gallons

Making an Estimate: Multiplication and Division

Practice

Here are three practice problems for you.

Quick-Solve 1

A hook-and-ladder fire truck can travel only 5 miles on one gallon of gasoline. In one year, the main fire truck in Morrowtown traveled 1,602 miles. About how many gallons of gasoline did it use that year?

Quick-Solve 2

Lasonya's pickup truck gets 14 miles to the gallon. She and her dad plan to travel 288 miles in the truck. About how many gallons of gas will they need?

Quick-Solve 3

On one trip, two men drove from San Francisco to New York City in about 39 hours. They drove 2,916 miles. Estimate their average speed. Hint: Speed can be calculated by dividing distance by time.

Applying Strategies

Use What You Know

The Sanchez family moved to a city 1,595 miles away. Mom drove the mini-van with the children and the dogs. The trip took 42 hours. About how many miles did she drive in one hour?

Look back to page 39 if you need help.

> Estimate by rounding the numbers for the time and distance. About how many miles did Mom drive in one hour?

1. Round each number to the nearest 10.

Actual	Estimated
1,595 miles traveled	about _____ miles traveled
42 hours traveled	about _____ hours traveled

2. Divide the estimates of total miles by the hours traveled.

about _____ miles per hour

3. The moving truck took 49 hours to make the trip. About how many miles per hour did it travel?

$$1{,}595 \div 49 =$$

about _____ ÷ _____ = about _____ miles per hour

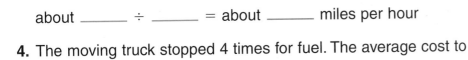

4. The moving truck stopped 4 times for fuel. The average cost to fill the 50-gallon tank was $52.25. About how much did the fuel for the truck cost for the whole trip?

_____

5. The mini-van stopped 6 times for fuel. The average cost to fill the tank was $27.91. About how much did the fuel for the mini-van cost for the whole trip? Did the fuel for the truck or for the mini-van cost more?

_____

Lesson 3   Solve Multi-Step Problems

You learned how to make an estimate to solve problems.
Now try solving this multi-step problem.

Six people are going to a concert. They will travel
a total of 336 miles to get there and back. They
want to spend as little as possible on gasoline. They
have a mini-van, a compact car, and a sports car available
for the trip. Which vehicle or vehicles should they choose?

Vehicle Type	Miles per Gallon	Passengers
mini-van	14 mpg	holds 8 people
compact car	28 mpg	holds 4 people
sports car	21 mpg	holds 2 people

1. For each vehicle, find how many gallons of gasoline is needed
   to drive to the concert.

Gallons of Gasoline Needed

Mini-Van	Compact Car	Sports Car
gallons $14\overline{)336}$ miles	gallons $28\overline{)336}$ miles	gallons $21\overline{)336}$ miles

2. What are two different ways that six people can go to
   the concert?

_____

3. Which vehicle or vehicles should they choose to use the least
   amount of gasoline?

_____

4. What if you estimate by rounding to the nearest 10? Would the
   result be the same? Explain why or why not.

_____

Solving Multi-Step Problems: Multiplication and Division

Practice

Here are three practice problems for you.

Quick-Solve 1

Michelle's family traveled 350 miles in 7 hours. Eric's family traveled 400 miles in 10 hours. Which family had the fastest average speed?

Quick-Solve 2

A truck and a car each traveled 210 miles. The truck used 15 gallons of gasoline. The car used 10 gallons of gasoline. How many miles can each vehicle travel on one gallon of gasoline? How do you know?

Quick-Solve 3

Ben's family drives past this highway sign. Their car's gasoline tank is $\frac{1}{4}$ full. A full tank holds 20 gallons of gasoline. The car gets 22 miles per gallon of gasoline. Should they take the next exit to buy gasoline? Estimate how much farther they can travel without stopping.

Use What You Know

Jonathan's car can travel 21 miles per gallon of gasoline. The gas tank holds 15 gallons. Juanita's sports-utility vehicle can travel only 13 miles for each gallon of gasoline. The gas tank on her vehicle holds 25 gallons. Whose vehicle can travel farther on one tank of gasoline? How much farther?

1. How far can Jonathan travel on one tank of gas?
   Show your work.

2. How far can Juanita travel on one tank of gas?
   Show your work.

3. Whose vehicle can travel farther on one tank of gas?
   How much farther?

4. Suppose that Jonathan and Juanita started at the same point and traveled in opposite directions. How far apart would they be when each had used 2 tanks of gas?

5. Suppose that gas cost $1.18 a gallon. If they both filled their tanks once, who paid more for gas? How much more?

Lesson 4 Solve It Your Way

Read each problem and decide how you will find the solution.

You may choose one of these strategies for each problem.

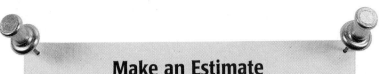

Make an Estimate
Solve Multi-Step Problems

1. A fire engine gets 5 miles to the gallon. It used 1,500 gallons of gas in one year and 1,700 gallons the following year. If gas cost the city $0.95 per gallon during both years, how much more did they spend in the second year?

2. Jack drove 72 miles on Monday, 74 miles on Tuesday, 88 miles on Wednesday, 91 miles on Thursday, and 84 miles on Friday. If he drove about the same distances the next week, what was his mileage total for two weeks?

3. A compact car gets 32 miles to the gallon. A mid-sized car gets 22 miles to the gallon. Which car can go more than 250 miles on 10 gallons of gas? How do you know?

4. Julie's station wagon gets 19 miles per gallon of gas. She has driven 120 miles. Has she used more than or less than 5 gallons of gas? How do you know?

5. It is 4:00 P.M. A concert begins at 8:30 P.M. Dave and his friends are 235 miles away from the concert. If they drive at 60 miles per hour, will they get to the concert in time?

6. Tom put 8 gallons of gas into his car. Gas costs $1.12 per gallon. Will a $20 bill be enough money to pay for 8 gallons? How do you know?

Application: Choosing a Strategy

Practice

Now write your own problems using multiplication and division.

Quick-Solve 1

The answer to a problem is "250 miles." What might the question be? Write your own problem to share with a friend. If your friend does not get an answer of 250 miles, discuss how you might change the problem or the solution to match.

Quick-Solve 2

The answer to a problem is "10 gallons of gas." What might the question be? Write your own problem to share with a friend. If your friend does not get an answer of 10 gallons of gas, discuss how you might change the problem or the solution to match.

Quick-Solve 3

The answer to a problem is "18 miles per gallon of gas." What might the question be? Write your own problem to share with a friend. If your friend does not get an answer of 18 miles per gallon of gas, discuss how you might change the problem or the solution to match.

Review   Show What You Know

Work in a small group. Help plan a beach vacation for 8 people. You will be gone 3 days. The beach is 140 miles away, or 280 miles round trip. You can rent a mini-van or two mid-sized cars. Suppose gasoline costs $1.23 per gallon. Would it be less expensive to choose the van or two mid-sized cars?

Vehicle Type	Miles per Gallon	Passengers	Rent per Day
Mini-Van	14 mpg	Holds 8 people	$45.00
Mid-Sized Car	22 mpg	Holds 4 people	$32.00

1. For one mini-van and for two mid-sized cars, find how many gallons of gasoline would be needed for the round trip. Then list how much the gasoline would cost.

Gallons of Gasoline Needed and the Cost

Vehicles	Total Gasoline	Cost of Gasoline
Mini-Van		
Two Mid-Sized Cars		

2. What is the total rental for one mini-van and for two cars?

One mini-van for 3 days = _____

Two mid-sized cars for 3 days = _____

3. Which vehicle or vehicles should they choose to spend the least total amount? How much money would they save?

_____

_____

UNIT 4 Pioneer Patterns

Lesson 1   Write a Plan

The students in the fifth grade are designing quilts as their projects for Pioneer Days. James and Dahlia's pattern makes up one of four squares of the quilt. How much red fabric do they need for each square?

Height = 6 in.

Base = 6 in.

Write a plan to solve the problem.

Step 1

Write in your own words what you need to find out.

_____

_____

Step 2

Write the facts that will be useful.

_____

_____

Step 3

Explain or show how you will solve the problem.

_____

_____

_____

_____

Writing a Plan: Area of Squares and Triangles

Solve a Simpler Problem

Try breaking the problem into simpler parts.

Find the area of the quilt square. Then find the area of the red and yellow portions of the square. How much red fabric will James and Dahlia need for each square?

Area is the number of square units that a figure covers.

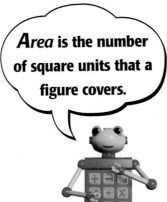

Height = 6 in.

Base = 6 in.

1. What shapes fit together to make the quilt square?

_____

2. What fraction of the square makes each shape? _____

3. To find the area of a square, multiply the base of the square times the height of the square. What is the area of the quilt

   square? _____ square inches

4. What is the area of the red triangle in the square? How do you know?

_____

_____

5. If the quilt has 4 of these squares, how much red fabric will James and Dahlia need?

_____

_____

_____

Practice

Here are three practice problems for you.

Quick-Solve 1
Two of the students in Mr. Burton's class are designing a quilt. How much blue fabric will they need to complete a design that has 12 squares like the one shown?

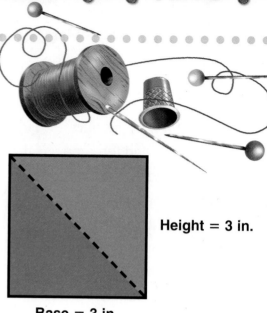

Height = 3 in.

Base = 3 in.

Quick-Solve 2
Pioneers heading west might have made a pinwheel design. What is the area of each triangle in this design? Hint: All of the squares are the same size.

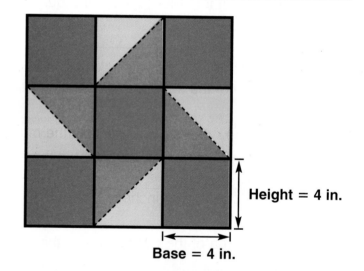

Height = 4 in.

Base = 4 in.

Quick-Solve 3
Jeremy chose to draw the Blockade design for his Pioneer Days project. What is the area of each purple triangle in his design?

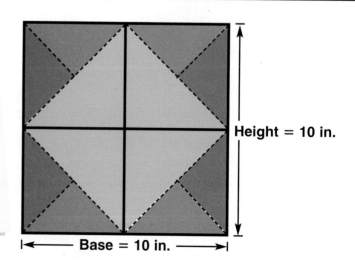

Height = 10 in.

Base = 10 in.

Use What You Know

The students want to make a banner with the school's colors. How much green fabric will they need?

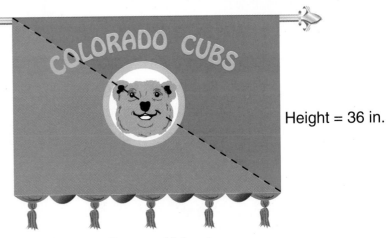

Height = 36 in.

Base = 48 in.

> Try breaking the problem into simpler parts to solve.

1. What shapes fit together to make the banner?

   _____

2. What fraction of the rectangle makes each shape? _____

3. To find the area of the banner, multiply the base times the height. What is the area of the banner?

   _____ square inches

4. How much green fabric will the students need? How do you know?

   _____

   _____

5. Janice began coloring a border design for a wall hanging.

   About how much area has she colored? _____

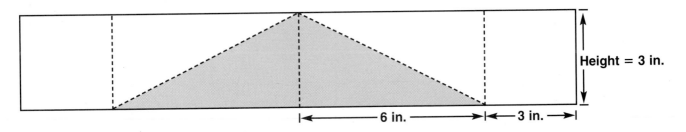

Height = 3 in.

6 in.   3 in.

Lesson 2   Write a Plan

Another class is making a quilt design for Pioneer Days. Their design will have a border that is made of parallelograms and triangles. What is the area of the purple parallelogram?

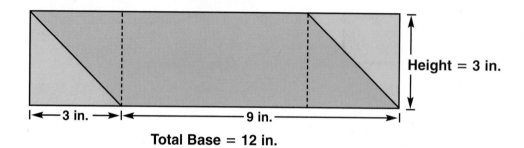

Height = 3 in.

|← 3 in. →|← 9 in. →|

Total Base = 12 in.

Write a plan to solve the problem.

Step 1   Write in your own words what you need to find out.

_____

_____

Step 2   Write the facts that will be useful.

_____

_____

Step 3   Explain or show how you will solve the problem.

_____

_____

_____

_____

_____

_____

Solve a Simpler Problem

Try breaking the problem into simpler parts.

> Notice that the purple parallelogram in the border
> design is made of 1 rectangle and 2 triangles. Find
> the area of the rectangle and triangles. Add them
> together to find the area of the parallelogram.

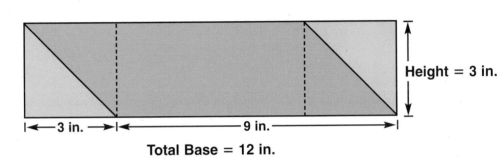

Height = 3 in.

|← 3 in. →|← ————— 9 in. ————— →|

Total Base = 12 in.

1. What is the area of the purple rectangle? _____ square inches

2. What is the area of each purple triangle? _____ square inches

3. What is the area of the parallelogram? How do you know?

_____

_____

_____

4. If there are 4 border pieces, how much purple fabric will the
   class need to complete the quilt?

_____

_____

_____

Practice

Here are three practice problems for you.

Quick-Solve 1

Camilla's quilt has a border with a parallelogram. How much green fabric will she need for the piece shown?

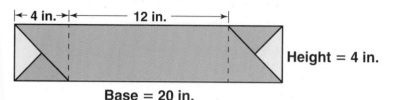

|← 4 in. →|← 12 in. →|

Height = 4 in.

Base = 20 in.

Quick-Solve 2

Juan's group designed a table runner for their Pioneer Days exhibit table. What is the area of the yellow portion of the table runner?

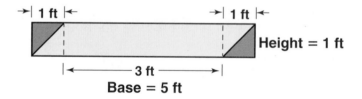

→| 1 ft |←   →| 1 ft |←

Height = 1 ft

|← 3 ft →|

Base = 5 ft

Quick-Solve 3

Mario's group made a quilted house design. How much fabric will they need for the gray roof piece?

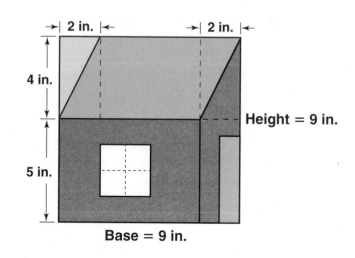

→| 2 in. |←   →| 2 in. |←

4 in.

Height = 9 in.

5 in.

Base = 9 in.

Use What You Know

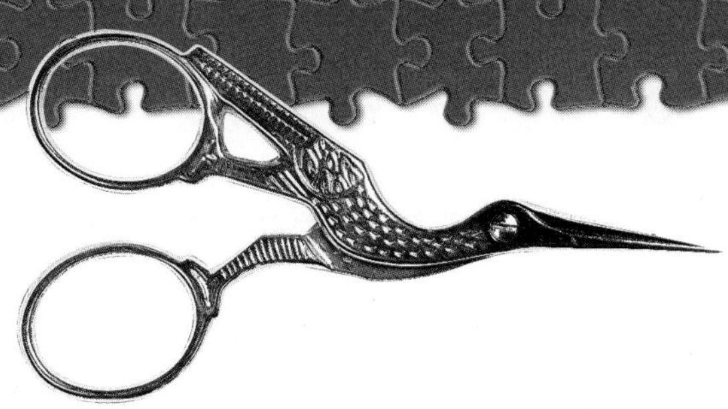

Leslie's group designed a chevron banner using parallelograms. How much blue fabric will they need?

Try breaking the problem into simpler parts to solve.

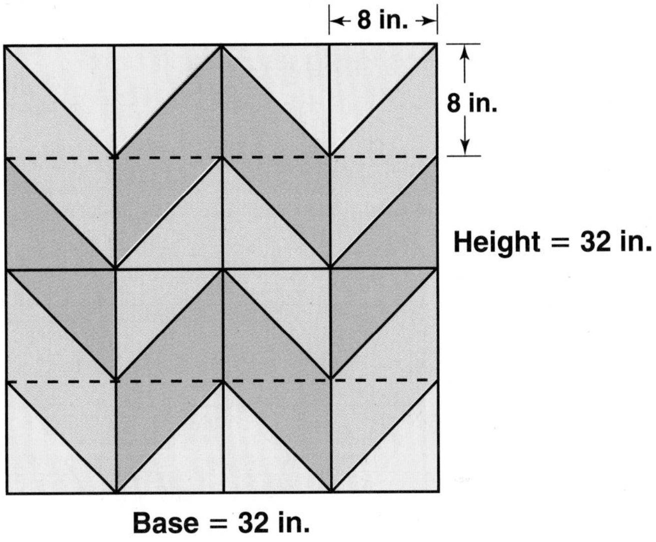
8 in.
8 in.
Height = 32 in.
Base = 32 in.

1. How many blue parallelograms are in the chevron design?

   _____ parallelograms

2. How many triangles make up each blue parallelogram?

   ____

3. What is the area of each blue triangle? _____ square inches

4. What is the area of each parallelogram? How do you know?

   ____

   ____

   ____

5. How much blue fabric will Leslie's group need to make the banner?

   ____

   ____

   ____

Lesson 3   Use a Formula

You have solved simpler problems to find area.
Now try using a formula.

> The formula to find the area of a parallelogram is: $A = (b \times h)$
>
> The formula to find the area of a triangle is: $A = (b \times h) \div 2$

Another class is designing a quilt border.
How much fabric will they need to make each
purple parallelogram and each yellow triangle?

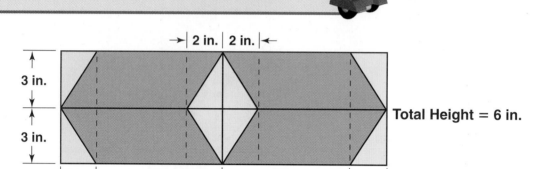

2 in. | 2 in.

3 in.

3 in.

Total Height = 6 in.

2 in. | 7 in. | 7 in. | 2 in.

Total Base = 18 in.

1. What is the length of the base of each parallelogram?

   _____ inches

2. What is the height of each parallelogram? _____ inches

3. Use the formula to find the area of each parallelogram.

   _____ × _____ = _____ square inches

4. Use the formula to find the area of each yellow triangle.

   _____ × _____ = _____ square inches

   _____ ÷ 2 = _____ square inches

5. How much purple fabric and yellow fabric will the class need to
   make the border for the entire quilt? Hint: The border will trim
   4 sides of the quilt.

   _____

   _____

Practice

Here are three practice problems for you.

Quick-Solve 1

Janice is making a pocketbook. How much fabric will she need for the purple flap?

Height = 8 in.

Base = 8 in.

Quick-Solve 2

Todd and his classmates are making chaps to wear in the Pioneer Days parade. How much dark brown suede is needed to decorate the chaps?

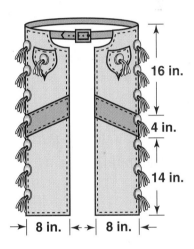

16 in.

4 in.

14 in.

8 in. | 8 in.

Quick-Solve 3

Natalie's group designed a crazy quilt. Will they use more green fabric or more blue fabric? Explain your answer.

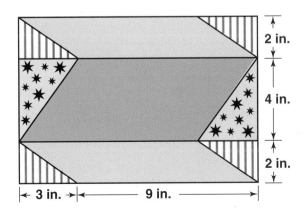

2 in.

4 in.

2 in.

3 in. | 9 in.

Use What You Know

If you need help, look back to page 56.

Sometimes quilts tell a story such as this one called Storm at Sea. How much fabric is needed to make each green parallelogram in the border and each blue triangle in the quilt?

> Try using a formula to solve.

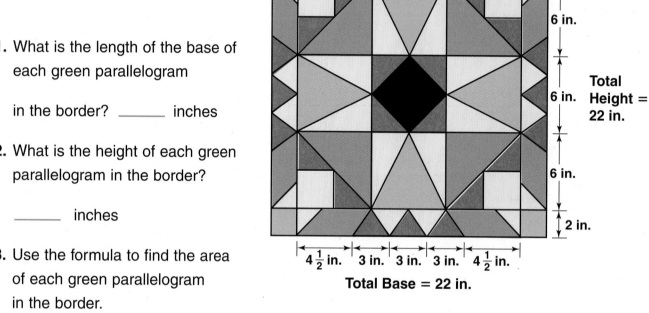

1. What is the length of the base of each green parallelogram

   in the border? _____ inches

2. What is the height of each green parallelogram in the border?

   _____ inches

3. Use the formula to find the area of each green parallelogram in the border.

   _____ × _____ = _____ square inches

4. Use the formula to find the area of each blue triangle.

   _____ × _____ = _____ square inches

   _____ ÷ 2 = _____ square inches

5. How much green fabric is needed to make the border of the quilt? How much blue fabric is needed for the triangles? How do you know?

   _____

   _____

Lesson 4   Solve It Your Way

Read each problem and decide
how you will find the solution.

You may want to choose one of these strategies for each problem.

Solve a Simpler Problem
Use a Formula

1. Tom's class made a quilt using the
   Shooting Star pattern shown. How
   much fabric did they use for each
   orange triangle?

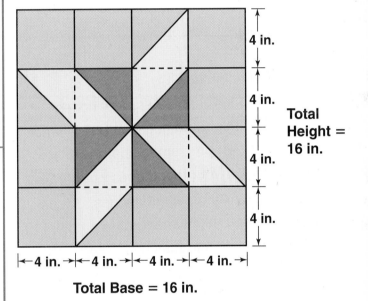

4 in.

4 in.

Total
Height =
16 in.

4 in.

4 in.

|← 4 in. →|← 4 in. →|← 4 in. →|← 4 in. →|

Total Base = 16 in.

2. How much fabric did they use for each
   yellow parallelogram?

3. A quilt for sale at Pioneer Days is made of
   4-inch by 4-inch squares. Each square is
   divided into two equal triangles. What is
   the area of each triangle?

4. The parallelogram part of a quilt square
   has a base of 6 inches and a height of
   4 inches. What is the area of the
   parallelogram?

Application: Choosing a Strategy

Practice

Now write your own problems about areas of triangles and parallelograms.

Quick-Solve 1

The answer is "10 square inches." What might the question be? Write your own problem to share with a friend. If your friend does not get an answer of 10 square inches, discuss how you might change the problem or the solution to match.

Quick-Solve 2

The answer is "12 square inches." What might the question be? Write your own problem to share with a friend. If your friend does not get an answer of 12 square inches, discuss how you might change the problem or the solution to match.

Quick-Solve 3

The answer is "72 square inches." What might the question be? Write your own problem to share with a friend. If your friend does not get an answer of 72 square inches, discuss how you might change the problem or the solution to match.

Review   Show What You Know

Work in a small group. Make a quilt design that uses triangles and parallelograms. Use at least two different colors.

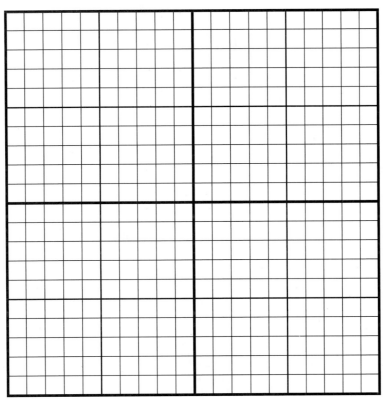

1. How many different shapes did you use? What is the area of each shape?

_____

_____

_____

2. Explain how you found the area of each shape. How much fabric would you need for each color?

_____

_____

_____

Read each problem and decide how you will find the solution.

Wow! You can choose from all these strategies!

**Make an Estimate
Solve Multi-Step Problems
Solve a Simpler Problem
Use a Formula**

1. Nick's car gets 26 miles on one gallon of gasoline. About how far can he drive on 9 gallons of gasoline?

2. A truck gets 12 miles per gallon of gasoline. Alda and Tina plan to travel 495 miles in the truck. About how many gallons of gasoline will they need?

3. Jenna's group designed the quilt shown. If each yellow triangle has a base of 6 inches and a height of 6 inches, how much yellow fabric is needed for all four?

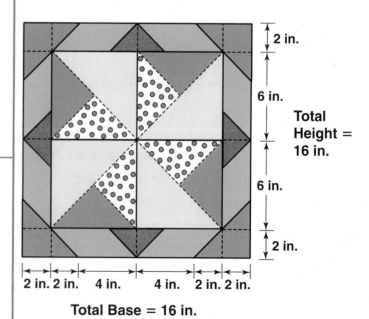

2 in.

6 in.

Total Height = 16 in.

6 in.

2 in.

2 in. 2 in.   4 in.   4 in.   2 in. 2 in.

Total Base = 16 in.

4. The border of the quilt has 8 parallelograms. What is the area of each parallelogram?

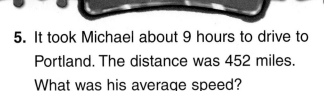

5. It took Michael about 9 hours to drive to Portland. The distance was 452 miles. What was his average speed?

6. The McCabe's family car gets about 18 miles to the gallon. Jane and her mom plan to travel 341 miles in the truck. About how many gallons of gas will they need?

7. How many square inches of fabric would you need to make the butterfly design?

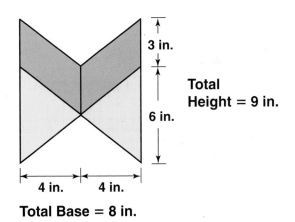

3 in.

6 in.

Total Height = 9 in.

4 in.   4 in.

Total Base = 8 in.

8. Mark's recreational vehicle gets 8 miles per gallon of gasoline. About how many gallons would it take to travel 234 miles?

9. Mrs. Chin's truck gets 8 miles to the gallon on average. Her tank holds 34 gallons of gasoline. Can she drive 300 miles on one tank of gas?

Data Detectives

Lesson 1 Write a Plan

The students in one class were told to collect data and present their findings in a graph. Jerry asked some students how they would spend $20.00. His graph is shown here. What fraction of the surveyed students would spend the money on videos?

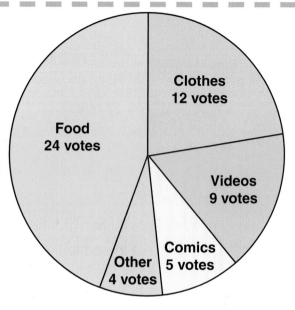

Write a plan to solve the problem.

Step 1 Write in your own words what you need to find out.

_____

_____

Step 2 Write the facts that will be useful.

_____

_____

Step 3 Explain or show how you will solve the problem.

_____

_____

_____

_____

_____

Use a Graph

Try using a circle graph to solve the problem.

Circle graphs are used to compare parts of a group to the whole group.

Look at the graph. What fraction of the students who were surveyed would spend the money on videos?

1. What does the whole circle represent?

_____

2. Use the circle graph to fill in the numbers in this list.

Food = _____ out of _____ students

Clothes = _____ out of _____ students

Videos = _____ out of _____ students

Comics = _____ out of _____ students

Other = _____ out of _____ students

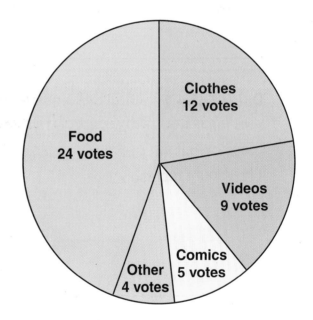

Food
24 votes

Clothes
12 votes

Videos
9 votes

Comics
5 votes

Other
4 votes

3. Explain how items in a list of data such as this can be changed to fractions.

_____

4. What fraction of the surveyed students would spend the

money on videos? Write the fraction in simplest form. _____

5. Now write all the other data as fractions in simplest form.

Food = _____   Clothes = _____   Comics = _____   Other = _____

Practice

Here are three practice problems for you.

Jenny completed a circle graph to show how the school spent money for a trip to the museum. Use the graph to answer the questions.

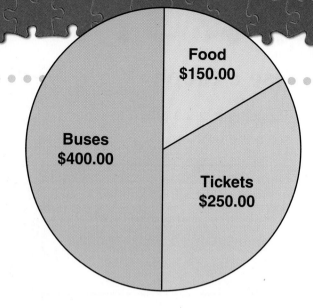

Quick-Solve 1

What was the total amount of money spent on the trip to the museum? How do you know?

Quick-Solve 2

How much money was spent on the buses? What fraction of the total does this amount represent?

Quick-Solve 3

The data in the graph represents 5 classes that went to the museum. If each class spent about the same amount on tickets, how much were the tickets for 1 class?

Use What You Know

Try using data from the graph to solve the problem.

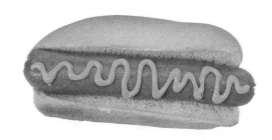

Javier decided to ask students to name their favorite lunch in the cafeteria. What fraction of the surveyed students chose tacos?

1. What does the whole circle represent?

_____

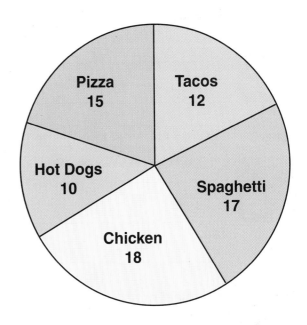

2. Use the circle graph to fill in the numbers in this list.

Hot Dogs = _____ out of _____ students

Pizza = _____ out of _____ students

Tacos = _____ out of _____ students

Spaghetti = _____ out of _____ students

Chicken = _____ out of _____ students

3. What fraction of the favorite lunches was tacos?

Write the fraction in simplest form. _____

4. Now write all the other data as fractions in simplest form.

Hot Dogs = _____   Pizza = _____   Spaghetti = _____   Chicken = _____

5. Look at the graph. Which two lunch choices combined won about half the votes for favorite lunches?

_____

Lesson 2   Write a Plan

Yvonne chose to survey some of the boys and girls in her school about their pets. She used a double bar graph to show her data. How many students in all have a dog or a cat?

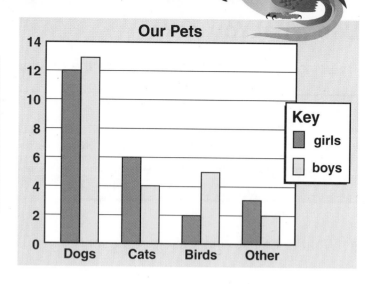

Our Pets

Key
■ girls
□ boys

Write a plan to solve the problem.

Step 1

Write in your own words what you need to find out.

_____

_____

Step 2

Write the facts that will be useful.

_____

_____

_____

Step 3

Explain or show how you will solve the problem.

_____

_____

_____

_____

_____

_____

Writing a Plan: Data and Statistics

Use a Graph

Double bar graphs are used to compare data about two surveyed groups.

Try using data from the graph to solve the problem.

Look carefully at Yvonne's graph. How many students in all have a dog or a cat?

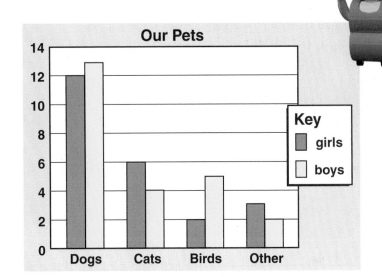

Our Pets

Key
- girls
- boys

1. Look at the graph key. How does it help you understand the data that is shown?

_____

2. What is the total number of boys surveyed? _____ boys

3. What is the total number of girls surveyed? _____ girls

4. How many students in all have a dog or a cat? Explain the steps you used to find the answer.

_____

_____

_____

5. How many girls have pets that are not dogs or cats? _____ girls

6. Why do you think Yvonne used *Other* in her graph?

_____

_____

Practice

Here are three practice problems for you.

Shari completed a double bar graph to show the type of music that students listen to. Use the graph to answer the questions.

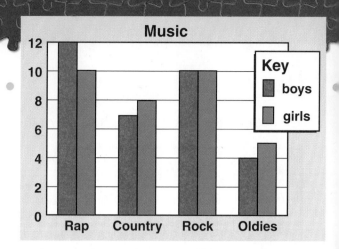

Quick-Solve 1

Were more votes counted from girls or from boys? How many more?

Quick-Solve 2

How many votes in all were for rap and for rock music? Is that greater than or less than the votes for country music and oldies all together? How do you know?

Quick-Solve 3

There were 44 students surveyed. The number of votes is greater than the number of students who were surveyed. Explain how this could be possible. Then find the difference between these numbers.

Applying Strategies

Use What You Know

Use what you know about graphs to solve problems.

Kyle asked 60 students if they had ever been in a play. If they had been in more than one, he asked them to pick their favorite role. His graph shows the roles students had in plays.

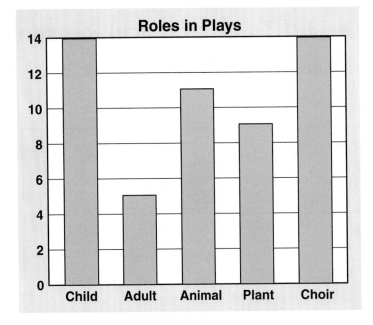

1. How many students have played

   the role of a person? _____ students

2. How many students in all have played the role of a

   plant or of an animal? _____ students

3. Some of the students answered that they had never been in a play. Kyle did not list these on his graph. How many students had an answer of *none?* How did you figure it out?

   _____

   _____

   _____

4. Look again at the total number of students who were surveyed. What is the fraction of students who have been in the choir of a play? How do you know?

   _____

   _____

   _____

Lesson 3   Use Logical Reasoning

You have used graphs to solve problems.
Now try using logical reasoning to solve a problem.

In a survey, Jon, Anita, and Sasha each were asked, "What is your favorite type of pizza?" Jon's answer won 10 more votes than Hamburger. Anita's choice was the least favorite. Sasha voted differently than Jon and Anita, but did not vote for Sausage. How did Jon, Anita, and Sasha answer?

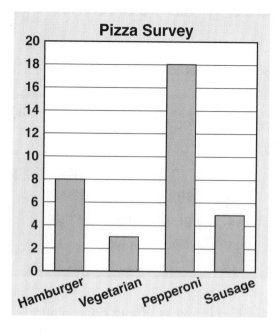

1. Every person who was surveyed voted once. How many people were surveyed? How do you know?

_____

2. Which pizza won 10 more votes than Hamburger?

_____

3. Which kind of pizza was the least favorite?

_____

4. Look at your answers so far and complete part of the chart below. Then read again the problem at the top of the page. Complete the rest of the chart to show how each person answered the survey.

Person	Pizza Preference
Jon	
Anita	
Sasha	

Using Logical Reasoning: Data and Statistics

Practice

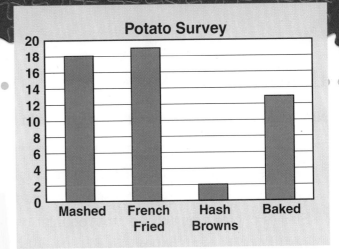

Potato Survey

Here are three practice problems for you.
Use the graph to answer the questions.

Quick-Solve 1

What are the categories of information shown in the graph? How many people voted?

Quick-Solve 2

Andrea and Jack were part of the survey on favorite potatoes. Andrea likes to eat her potatoes with a hamburger at a fast-food restaurant. Jack's favorite potato style got one less vote than Andrea's choice. How did each of them vote?

Quick-Solve 3

Samuel, Maggie, and Frank each voted differently on favorite ways to have potatoes. Frank won't eat anything fried. Samuel agreed with one fourth of the votes. None of them voted for the least favorite style. How did each of them vote?

Use What You Know

Now try another problem that uses logic with a graph.

Emily's class had a party. Each student voted once for the kind of party he or she wanted. Emily's choice was not the most popular or the least favorite, but it got more votes than Jan's. Jan's choice was not the least favorite. Ian's vote was not the most popular answer. How did Emily, Jan, and Ian vote if they voted three different ways?

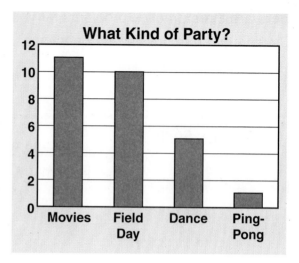

1. How many students are in Emily's class? How do you know?

_____

2. What are the possible ways Emily might have voted?

_____

3. If Jan's choice was not the least favorite, how does that help you know how Emily voted?

_____

_____

4. How did Emily and Jan vote?

Emily _____ Jan _____

5. How did Ian vote? How do you know? Why must you know how Emily and Jan voted before you can know Ian's answer?

_____

_____

_____

Lesson 4   Solve It Your Way

Read each problem and decide how you
will find the solution.

You may choose one
of these strategies for
each problem.

Use a Graph
Use Logical Reasoning

Robert surveyed his classmates to find their favorite
outdoor summer activity. Each student voted only
once. Use his graph if you need to.

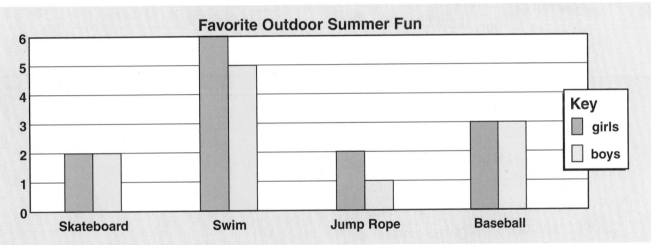

Favorite Outdoor Summer Fun

Key
■ girls
□ boys

Skateboard   Swim   Jump Rope   Baseball

---

1. How many students did Robert survey for
   his graph?

2. Were there more boys or more girls
   surveyed? How many more?

---

3. Lisa voted for an activity that had the
   same number of votes from girls as it had
   from boys. It uses something round that is
   not wheels. What was Lisa's vote?

4. One more girl than boy voted the same
   way as Clint. Kevin and Clint voted for the
   same activity. How did Clint and Kevin
   vote? How do you know?

Application: Choosing a Strategy

Practice

Now write your own problems using the circle graph or bar graph.

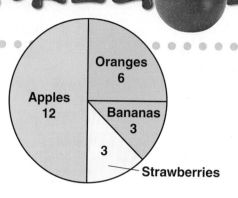

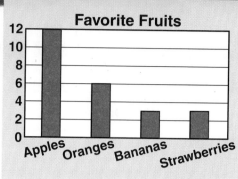

Quick-Solve 1

The answer to a problem is "one-half the people surveyed." What might the question be? Write your own problem to share with a friend. If your friend does not get an answer of one-half, discuss how you might change the problem or the solution to match.

Quick-Solve 2

The answer to a problem is "6 people." What might the question be? Write your own problem to share with a friend. If your friend does not get an answer of 6, discuss how you might change the problem or the solution to match.

Quick-Solve 3

The answer to a problem is "3 people." What might the question be? Write your own problem to share with a friend. If your friend does not get an answer of 3, discuss how you might change the problem or the solution to match.

Applying Strategies

Review   Show What You Know

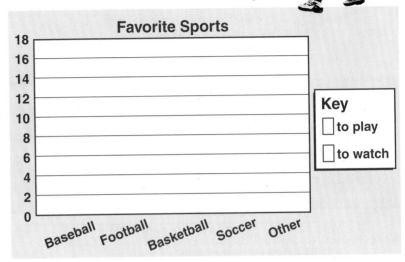

Work in a small group to complete your own survey and graph.

As a group, ask people their favorite sport to play and their favorite sport to watch. Allow them one vote for each question. Then complete the double-bar graph and color key.

Favorite Sports

18
16
14
12
10
8
6
4
2
0

Baseball   Football   Basketball   Soccer   Other

Key
☐ to play
☐ to watch

1. How many people did you survey? ———

2. Did more people choose to *play* baseball

   or to *watch* baseball? ———

3. Did you need to use the *Other* category on the graph? How does that category help a survey?

_____

_____

4. Now try to make a circle graph that shows how many people in all voted for each sport.

Surprise Supplies

Lesson 1   Write a Plan

Ms. Spinoza keeps a supply of fancy erasers in her desk to give her students for their good work. She needs 3 more erasers to have enough for everyone. She buys 3 erasers for $0.27 each. How much does she spend?

Write a plan to solve the problem.

Step 1   Write in your own words what you need to find out.

_____

_____

Step 2   Write the facts that will be useful.

_____

_____

_____

Step 3   Explain or show how you will solve the problem.

_____

_____

_____

_____

_____

Writing a Plan: Multiplying Decimals

Make a Model

Try making a model to solve the problem.

Sometimes a model can help you see how a problem works.

The model grid has 100 squares with 27 of them shaded. It represents 27 out of 100, which can be stated $\frac{27}{100}$ or 0.27. Use the second grid to show how much 3 erasers cost at $0.27 each.

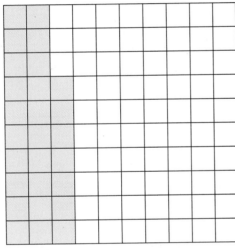

$0.27

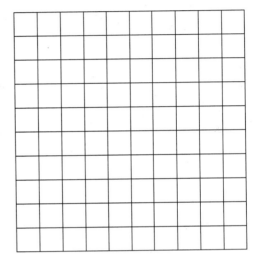

$0.27 × 3

1. Think of 0.27 as 2 tenths and 7 hundredths. The model already shows this figure once. Shade the second grid to show 0.27 times 3.

2. Look at the model you have shaded. Write the number of tenths and hundredths shown. Then regroup and write the tenths and hundredths again.

   _____ tenths _____ hundredths = _____ tenths _____ hundredths

3. How much did Ms. Spinoza spend for 3 erasers that cost $0.27 each? Was it more than or less than one dollar? How do you know?

   _____

   _____

Practice

Here are three practice problems for you.

Quick-Solve 1

Cara buys 2 rulers for $0.49 each. How much does she spend in all?

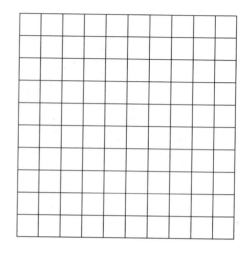

Quick-Solve 2

Paulo buys 5 stickers for $0.13 each. How much does he spend in all?

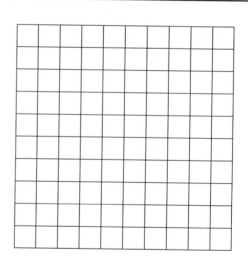

Quick-Solve 3

Mr. Tsui buys 4 erasers for $0.27 each. How much more than $1.00 does he spend? How do you know?

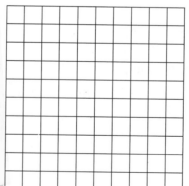
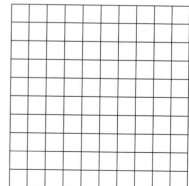

Applying Strategies

Use What You Know

Try making a model to solve the problem.

Emily wants to give her best friend a small present. She buys 2 pens that cost $0.38 each. How much does she spend?

The number of decimal places in the product is the same as the total number of decimal places in the factors.

1. Think of 0.38 as 3 tenths and 8 hundredths. Shade the grid to show 0.38 times 2.

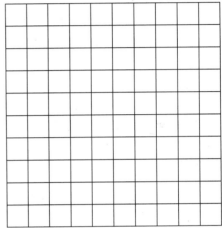

2. Look at the model you have shaded. Write the number of tenths and hundredths shown. Then regroup and write the tenths and hundredths again.

_____ tenths _____ hundredths = _____ tenths _____ hundredths

3. How much does Emily spend for 2 pens that cost $0.38 each? Is the total amount more than or less than one dollar? How do you know?

_____

_____

4. What if Emily wanted to buy 3 pens for $0.38 each? Would you need more than one grid to shade enough hundredths to show 0.38 × 3? How do you know?

_____

_____

Making a Model: Multiplying Decimals

Lesson 2 Write a Plan

Mr. Wong's class entered a writing contest. Two of his students tied for first place. Mr. Wong bought each of them a spiral notebook to show that he was proud of them. The notebooks were $0.91 each. How much did Mr. Wong spend?

Write a plan to solve the problem.

Step 1 Write in your own words what you need to find out.

_____

_____

Step 2 Write the facts that will be useful.

_____

_____

_____

Step 3 Explain or show how you will solve the problem.

_____

_____

_____

_____

_____

_____

_____

Writing a Plan: Multiplying Decimals

Make a Model

Try making a model to solve the problem.

> The notebooks were $0.91 each. How much did Mr. Wong spend to buy 2 of them? Show $0.91 on both grids. Then count the total number of tenths and hundredths in all.

Think of these facts:
100 pennies = $1.00
10 dimes = $1.00

1. Shade each grid to represent $0.91.

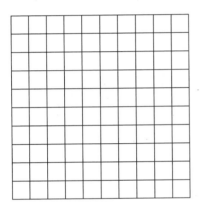 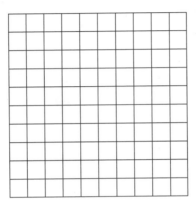

2. Count the total number of tenths and hundredths shaded.

_____ tenths   _____ hundredths

3. Regroup. Remember that 10 tenths equals 1 whole. Then restate the answer as a dollar amount with a decimal.

_____ ones _____ tenths _____ hundredths = $_____

4. What if notebooks cost $0.80 each? How much would 2 of them cost together? To show the answer on these grids, fill one grid completely before starting the next. Think of the number of tenths in $0.80 to do this.

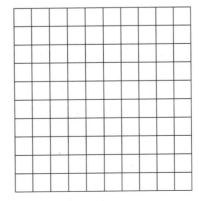

Practice

Here are three practice problems for you.

Quick-Solve 1

Miss Anderson bought 2 spiral notebooks for the writing champions in her class. She used a discount coupon, so the notebooks cost her only $0.77 each. How much did she spend?

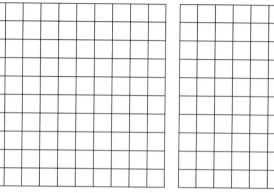

Quick-Solve 2

Charles bought some stickers to put on his writing notebook. He bought 6 stickers that were $0.25 each. How much did he spend in all?

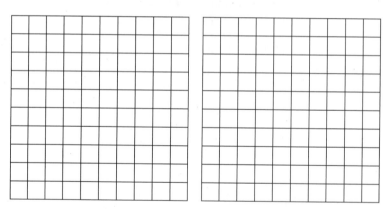

Quick-Solve 3

Denise has $2.00 to spend on pencils. She chooses some pencils that cost $0.53 each. Does she have enough money to buy 4 of them?

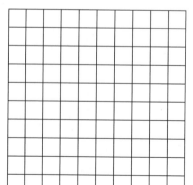
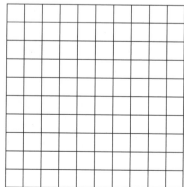

Applying Strategies

Use What You Know

Use what you know about making a model to solve problems.

You can show how to divide decimals by making a model.

> Leisha spent $1.88 to buy 2 spiral notebooks. How much did each notebook cost?

1. Shade the grids to represent $1.88.

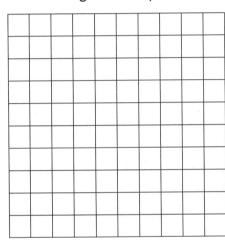 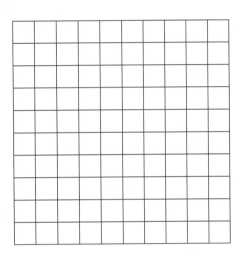

2. What is the total number of tenths shaded? _____ tenths

3. Since Leisha bought 2 notebooks, divide the number of tenths by 2. Then circle half of the tenths on the grid.

How many tenths did you circle? _____ tenths

4. Now do the same for the hundredths. Circle half of the hundredths. How many did you circle? _____ hundredths

5. Look at the number of tenths and hundredths that represent $1.88 divided by 2. Write an amount to show how much Leisha spent on each notebook

_____ tenths _____ hundredths = $_____

Lesson 3 Choose the Operation

You have made models to solve problems.
Now try choosing the operation to solve problems.

Remember: To place the decimal in a product, count the decimal places in the factors.

> Mrs. Marsh bought fancy pencils to give each of her 24 students. The pencils cost $0.96 each. If each student got one pencil, what was the total cost of the pencils?

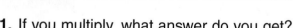

1. If you multiply, what answer do you get?

$$\begin{array}{r} \$0.96 \\ \times\ 24 \\ \hline \end{array}$$

2. If you divide, what answer do you get?

$$24\overline{)\$0.96}$$

3. Is it more reasonable to multiply or to divide to solve the problem? How do you know?

_____

4. What was the total cost of the pencils? $_____

5. What if Mrs. Marsh bought 30 pencils? If the price per pencil is the same, how much will she spend this time?

Show how you find the solution. $_____

Choosing the Operation: Mixed Operations with Decimals

Practice

Here are three practice problems for you.

Quick-Solve 1

Mr. Nash buys a set of shells and stars to give his students for working hard. There are 48 items in the set. The set cost $5.28. How much does each item cost?

Quick-Solve 2

Ms. Ellis buys a set of plastic bugs to give her students for working hard. There are 84 bugs in the set. The set cost $4.20. How much does each bug cost?

Quick-Solve 3

Dexter was awarded 15 gold star stickers and 3 fancy erasers for working hard in his class one year. Each sticker is worth $0.13. Each eraser is worth $0.27. What is the value of Dexter's awards?

Use What You Know

Mr. Abramson uses mini dinosaurs to award his students. A package of dinosaurs costs him $10.08. There are 72 dinosaurs in a package. What is the price of each dinosaur?

If a number with a decimal is divided by a whole number, the quotient will have a decimal in the same place.

1. If you multiply, what answer do you get?

$$\begin{array}{r} \$10.08 \\ \times \quad 72 \\ \hline \end{array}$$

2. If you divide, what answer do you get?

$$72\overline{)\$10.08}$$

3. Is it more reasonable to multiply or to divide to solve the problem? How do you know?

_____

4. What is the cost of each dinosaur? $ _____

5. What if Mr. Abramson bought a package of 108 dinosaurs? If the price per dinosaur is the same, how much will he spend this time?

Show how you find the solution. $ _____

Choosing the Operation: Mixed Operations with Decimals

Lesson 4   Solve It Your Way

Read each problem and decide how you will find the solution.

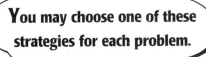

You may choose one of these strategies for each problem.

Make a Model
Choose the Operation

1. Tyrone bought 2 packages of notebook paper. Each package cost $0.89. How much did Tyrone spend on the paper?

2. Miss Craft bought 3 pairs of scissors for a group art project. Each pair cost $0.99. How much did she spend on the scissors?

3. Shannon won 20 gold stars in a year! If each star is worth $0.26, what is the value of the stars that Shannon was awarded?

4. Ms. Alvarez bought 5 identical sets of math Bingo games for her class to use. She spent $58.75. How much did each set cost?

5. Mr. Washington bought 3 sets of fraction pieces to use on his overhead projector. He spent a total of $22.77. What was the cost of each set?

6. Mrs. Mendelson wanted to order rubber bands and geoboards. She can get 350 rubber bands for $2.95 or 450 rubber bands for $4.75. Which is the better deal? Hint: Find the price per rubber band in each package.

Practice

Now write your own problems using multiplication and division.

Quick-Solve 1

The answer to a problem is "$0.85." What might the question be? Write your own problem to share with a friend. If your friend does not get an answer of $0.85, discuss how you might change the problem or the solution to match.

Quick-Solve 2

The answer to a problem is "6 mini dinosaurs." What might the question be? Write your own problem to share with a friend. If your friend does not get an answer of 6, discuss how you might change the problem or the solution to match.

Quick-Solve 3

The answer to a problem is "$3.18." What might the question be? Write your own problem to share with a friend. If your friend does not get an answer of $3.18, discuss how you might change the problem or the solution to match.

Applying Strategies

Review   Show What You Know

Work in a group to collect prices of school supplies.

In a group of 2 to 4 people, find out what the school supplies
listed below cost. You may look for newspaper ads, get prices
from a store, or look for prices in a school supply catalog.
Then use the information to find out what the total cost would
be to buy everyone in your group 1 of every item on the list.

1. Find a catalog or store price for each of these items:

   notebook paper $_____

   pencil $_____

   ink pen $_____

   thin spiral notebook $_____

2. How many people are in your group? _____ people

3. Is it more reasonable to multiply or to divide to solve the problem?
   Will you also need to add or to subtract? How do you know?

   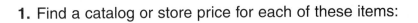

4. Explain two ways that you can find the total cost of the
   school supplies for all the people in your group.

   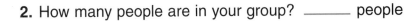

5. What is the total cost for everyone in your group to buy
   1 of every item on the list? Show your work.

Review Units 5–6

Read each problem and decide how you will find the solution.

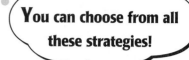
You can choose from all these strategies!

> **Use a Graph**
> **Use Logical Reasoning**
> **Make a Model**
> **Choose the Operation**

1. Shelly bought some felt tip pens for her art class. The pens were sold in a package of 12 for $6.36. What was the price of each pen?

2. Ms. Rodgers bought piano stickers for 18 music students. The stickers are sold in sheets of 12 stickers per sheet for $1.56. Is $3.50 enough money to pay for the amount of stickers she needs in order to give one to each student?

3. Logan asked the students in his class to vote for their favorite book topic. Look at the graph. How many students did Logan survey?

4. What fraction of the surveyed students enjoy reading mysteries?

5. Logan reported that half as many students read sports books as science fiction. Is he correct? How do you know?

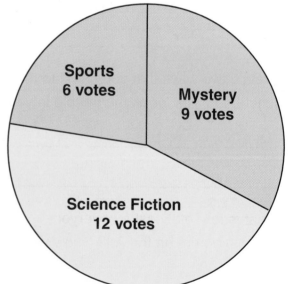

Favorite Book Topics

Sports
6 votes

Mystery
9 votes

Science Fiction
12 votes

6. Jerry wants to buy 4 toy dinosaurs at $0.23 each. Is one dollar enough to pay for the dinosaurs?

7. Mr. Dodson wants to order binoculars for his science class. Each pair of binoculars costs $2.95. If he buys a set of 10, Mr. Dodson would pay $27.50. How much money will he save if he buys the set?

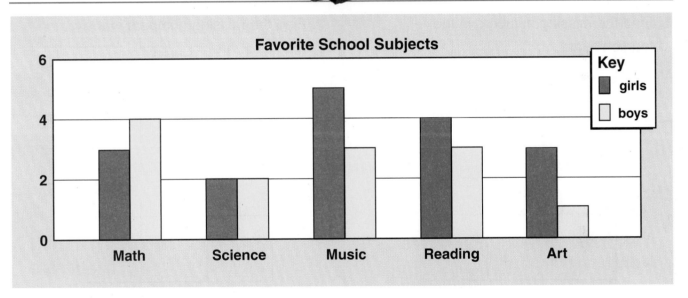

8. Barbara asked her classmates to vote for their favorite school subjects. Look at her bar graph. How many students were surveyed? What fraction of Barbara's class enjoy math and music the most?

9. Carla's favorite subject won half as many votes as Jan's, but she did not vote for Art. Todd was the only boy to vote for his favorite subject. How did each of them vote?

Final Review

Wow! Now you can choose from all these strategies!

Read each problem and decide how you will find the solution.

Work Backward
Choose the Operation
Make an Estimate
Use a Formula
Make a Model

Use Logical Reasoning
Solve Multi-Step Problems
Solve a Simpler Problem
Use a Graph

1. Find the missing numbers in the magic square.

13	2	21
3	22	11

2. Find the missing numbers in the magic square.

12		8
	9	
10		6

3. The sum of this magic square is 24. Find the missing numbers.

11		9
	8	

4. The sum of this magic square is 123. Find the missing numbers.

47		
	41	
	37	

5. In 1783, the Harper family paid $3,660.00 for 6 square miles of frontier land. How much did they pay for each square mile?

6. The Wilder family bought 4 acres of frontier land for $585.00 per acre. The next year, they bought 2 acres for $600.00 each. How much did they spend in all?

7. Anton's modern sports car can run about 19 miles on each gallon of gasoline. Anton wants to take a trip to a city that is 194 miles away. About how much gasoline will he need to get there? About how much gasoline will he need for the round trip?

8. Mrs. Cook drives a van of children to camp each year. She uses about 28 gallons of gasoline for the trip. One summer the gasoline cost $1.03 per gallon. The next summer, the price had jumped to $1.29 per gallon. About how much more did she spend that summer?

9. Mrs. Lopez is making a quilt for her daughter. How much green fabric will she need to make 12 squares like the one shown?

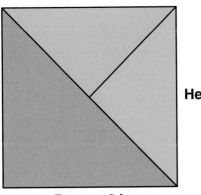

Height = 6 in.

Base = 6 in.

10. James is making a quilt with 16 squares like the one shown. How much gray fabric will he need for his quilt?

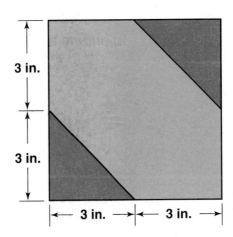

3 in.

3 in.

3 in. 3 in.

Kristy surveyed some of the students in her school to find out their favorite colors. Each student voted once. Use Kristy's graph to answer questions 11 and 12.

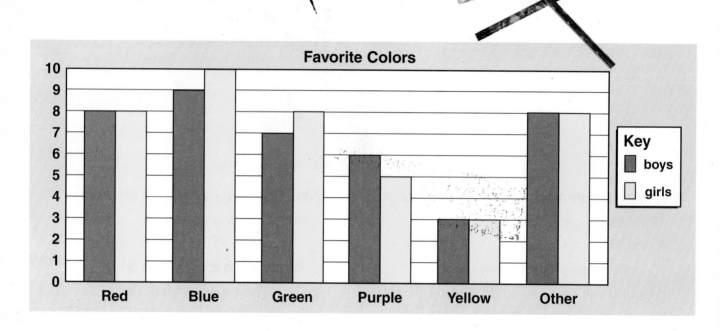

Favorite Colors

Key
■ boys
□ girls

11. How many girls in all voted for a favorite color? How many boys in all voted?

12. Ben and Cece voted the same way. One more girl than boy voted for the color Ben chose. Cece did not vote for green. What color did Ben and Cece choose?

13. Phil bought 4 erasers to put on his pencils. They cost $0.19 each. How much did Phil spend?

14. Miss Hill bought 29 fancy pencils to give her students. She spent a total of $22.91. If each pencil cost the same amount, what was the price per pencil?

Cumulative Review: Applying Strategies